WORLD WAR I

igloobooks

igloobooks

Published in 2016
by Igloo Books Ltd
Cottage Farm
Sywell
NN6 0BJ
www.igloobooks.com

LEO002 1016
2 4 6 8 10 9 7 5 3 1
ISBN 978-1-78670-259-3

Cover image: The Print Collector / © Alamy Stock Photo

Cover designed by Simon Parker
Edited by Bobby Newlyn-Jones

Printed and manufactured in China

Contents

Introduction

At the start of the 20th Century, the political map of Europe was dominated by old allegiances and Empires. The Ottoman Empire, nicknamed, the 'Sick Old Man of Europe,' was crumbling, leading to questions of who would govern the lands and peoples that it could no longer govern.

British troops go forward in 'No Man's Land', Battle of the Somme, 1916

To the West, Britain ruled the seas and governed swathes of territory around the world. This made it powerful but also created animosity among its European neighbours, especially Germany.

Other great changes were taking place. Every nation was relying more heavily on industry. Planes were a new invention but their technology was advancing rapidly. Huge ocean-going liners made faster and faster journeys from one continent to another, enabling the swifter spread of ideas and populations.

In warfare, the machine gun was transforming the concept of battle from man-to-man combat to a situation in which one man could kill hundreds within minutes.

In short, the speed of change and the growth of tension had created a dry tinder box which only needed the tiniest of sparks to ignite into all-out aggression. On June 28th 1914 the spark came in the form of an assassination. The assassination of Archduke Franz Ferdinand of Austria was no more than an excuse to fight, but it was the only excuse that was needed. From the actions of one young assassin came a war so bloody, terrible and extensive that it changed the concept of war forever. It became known to us as the Great War.

Gavrilo Princip arrested after assassinating Archduke Franz Ferdinand in Sarajevo, Bosnia, 28 June 1914

Gassed, inspired by John Singer Sargent's time on the front line; it depicts a side on view of a line of soldiers being led along a duckboard by a medical orderly; their eyes are bandaged as a result of exposure to gas and each man holds on to the shoulder of the man in front

WORLD WAR ONE

British troops moving up to the trenches, 2.5 miles East of Ypres

How the Trigger was Pulled

In the years prior to World War I, the political map of Europe was quite different from the present era. Some of the countries we know today were still evolving in terms of their territorial boundaries and ethnic tensions were running high in central and eastern regions.

At the heart of this area was the Austro-Hungarian Empire, which comprised lands that are now recognized as, all or part of, no fewer than fourteen countries. Naturally, the ethnic minority populations disliked having their lands held by the Empire and they disliked the regime of oppression placed on their peoples, from the Austrians and the Hungarians.

Franz Ferdinand (1863 - 1914),
Archduke of Austria, heir-apparent
to the emperor Franz Joseph

A Bosnian Serb, named Gavrilo Princip, had enough of living under the empirical thumb. He joined a nationalist paramilitary movement named the Black Hand, whose ambition it was to fight for Serbian independence.

In June 1914, Princip and his comrades learnt that the heir to the Austro-Hungarian throne, Archduke Franz Ferdinand, would be making an official visit to Sarajevo, so they hatched a plot to assassinate him in the name of their cause. On the 28th the Black Hand prepared to carry out their plan, but things went wrong and the Archduke escaped unharmed. However, following the visit his driver took a backstreet to avoid the possibility of a further attempt on the Archduke's life.

It just so happened that the dejected Princip was walking along that very same backstreet. He immediately seized his opportunity and shot both the Archduke and his wife at close range. The job was done, but Princip could not imagine the chain of events he had started by succeeding in assassinating the Archduke.

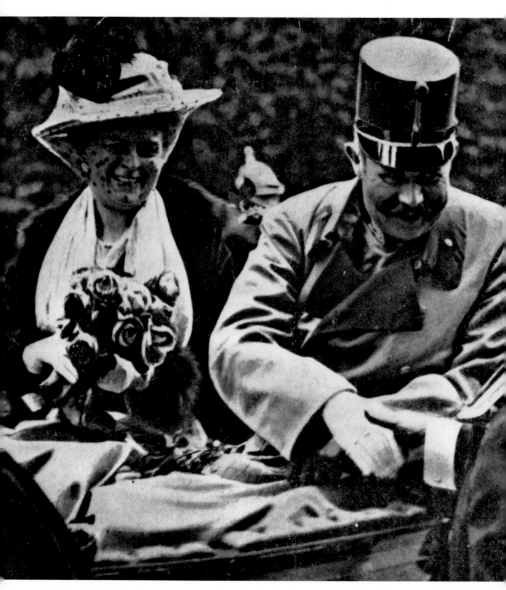

The Archduke and his wife, Sophie, shortly
before their assassination in Sarajevo

The Australasians wanted to take their revenge on the Serbian kingdom, amassed troops on the border and declared war. This prompted much political manoeuvring among the powers of Europe, according to historical allegiances. Just a month after the assassination, the entire sub-continent was poised for war as all parties took their sides.

As for Princip, he languished in prison for the next few years, where he eventually died from tuberculosis some months before World War I came to a close. His dream of an independent Serbia would not become a reality until the end of the 20th century and the region remains in a state of political tension due to ethnic divisions and political schisms. The Austro-Hungarian Empire was officially dissolved on the 31st October, 1918, eleven days before the official ceasefire of The Great War.

Serbian student Gavrilo Princip, who assassinated Franz Ferdinand

Taking Sides

In the month following the assassination of Archduke Franz Ferdinand, the European nations took sides in preparation for all-out war, on a scale never seen before. The British Empire allied with the French and Russian Empires, to form the Triple Entente. The Austro-Hungarian Empire joined with the German Empire to form the Central Powers. The German ruler, Kauster Willhelm II was ambitious and nationalistic and encouraged Austria towards war.

A number of other European nations remained neutral, as they either had no vested interest in going to war, or they had no bellicose inclinations. They included the countries of the Iberian Peninsula, Scandinavia and South-eastern Europe. Serbia and Montenegro allied with the Russian Empire as part of the Entente. Switzerland remained neutral despite being in the middle of the war zone.

King Carol I of Romania from 1881. At the beginning of World War I he declared Romania neutral

Front page of French newspaper Le Petit Journal: Death to the Monster
– France, England, Serbia, Russia and Belgium have declared war on
Germany and Austria

As the key participants of the Entente and the Central Powers were empires, this meant that they each possessed territories and populations in other parts of the world. Although most of the fighting would take place in Europe, those involved were from a truly international collection of colonies, from all five continents. This is why it became known as the First World War, as opposed to The European War. Many described it as The Great War, until World War II superseded it in terms of scale.

Unfortunately for the Central Powers, their combined empires were far smaller than those of the Entente, which immediately gave them a disadvantage, both in terms of material resources and available personnel. Despite the clear likelihood that they would ultimately lose the war, they chose to commence hostilities on the 28th July 1914. It seems that a combination of Teutonic pride and imperial ambition gave the enemy an over-inflated idea of their destiny, leaving them hell-bent on expanding their realm on the map of Europe and on the map of the World as a consequence of conquest.

The famous World War I
recruiting poster featuring
Lord Kitchener

"YOUR COUNTRY NEEDS
YOU"

A recruitment drive during
the First World War at
Trafalgar Square, London

Army recruits taking the oath at offices in White City, 1914

Blind Enthusiasm

A good deal of discussion has been conducted over the fact that most British soldiers volunteered to go to war in the initial stages. That is to say, conscription was not really required, because so many British men were enthusiastic about the idea of becoming soldiers and serving their country. So enthusiastic, in fact, that those considered too young to fight would often pretend to be older, and those considered too old would often pretend to be younger.

This blind enthusiasm seems to have resulted from a combination of factors in British society at that time in history. For one thing, very few people had first-hand experience of warfare in the Edwardian period, so most had little idea of the true horrors awaiting them. In addition, Britain was a rather staid and predictable environment, so the idea of adventure abroad was a very inviting prospect. There was also a strong sense of belonging to the great empire, so that men wanted to play their part in the war for fear of being seen of in a negative light by society.

Group photo, British
soldiers, WW1

Your Chums are Fighting
Why aren't YOU?
No. 2 Central Recruiting Committee, No. 2 Military Division, Toronto
Stone Ltd

It is also important to remember that there was a very clear class structure in Britain as a hangover from the Victorian era. The working class had laborious lives of subservience, repetition and drudgery. The middle class had tedious lives of pen pushing and managerial duties. The upper class had idle lives of hunting and sporting in imitation of true challenge. Not surprisingly, men from all three classes were excited by the prospect of donning uniforms and going overseas to give the enemy their dues.

In their minds it amounted to an adventure holiday, firing guns and enjoying a macho environment for a few months, before returning home with something to talk about for the rest of their lives. Very few seem to have had any real notion that there would be no more of their lives to enjoy. This was compounded by the propaganda used to invite them to war in the first place and the notion that warfare was no longer a matter of hand-to-hand combat, but rather something conducted over a civilized distance between friend and foe.

British Army recruitment poster, 1917

After eighteen months of fighting, the reality of modern warfare had become clear. So many men had been slaughtered on the killing fields that conscription was introduced for all men between the ages of 18 and 41 with the Military Service Act 1916. By 1918, the upper-age parameter had been raised to 51 years in order to compensate for the woeful losses on the Western Front. A young army had been all but replaced by a middle aged army.

British soldiers in the trenches during World War I, 1914

Infantrymen sitting in a trench
reading and smoking during the
early days of trench warfare

37

Entrenchment

When World War I broke out, on 28th July 1914, the Central Powers launched a campaign to reach the English Channel by advancing into France. This became known as the Race to the Sea and followed a number of opening battles in the war. These included the Battle of the Marne and the Battle of the Aisne. The original intention of the German Imperial Army had been to take Paris but this ambition had been thwarted by the Allies, so the Germans tried a new tactic.

As the Germans tried to fight their way to the coast, the French and British forces resisted. Many subsequent attacks and counter-attacks eventually led to a stalemate situation in the region of Artois and Flanders. The result was a more-or-less static frontline between the opposing forces. So it was, that the Western Front became a north-south line, stretching from Nieuport in Belgium down towards Paris in France.

Due to the stasis, both sides were forced to settle into a prolonged trench war. Once in a while, offensives and counter-offensives would move the frontline westward and eastward, but never any considerable distance. This meant that the same swathe of fighting terrain was occupied for about four years. As a consequence, the landscape became a featureless expanse of mud as hundreds of thousands of shells destroyed the trees and ploughed the soil with their explosions. Buildings and roads suffered the same treatment, so that the battlegrounds became panoramas in shades of brown, with little to distinguish one place from another, save the odd ruin, tree stump, hill or stream.

View of almost totally destroyed town; crude sign reads, "this was Forges" (possibly Forges-les-Eaux)

With every feature razed to the ground, it also meant nowhere to hide. The only option, for both sides, was to live a subterranean existence in trenches, tunnels and dugouts. Conditions were unpleasant to say the least. Not only did soldiers have to contend with unsanitary and damp conditions, but the land around them was strewn with the decomposing fragments of corpses. The winters brought constant muddy wetness and cold, while the summers brought the stench of putrefaction.

Then there were the animal pests to deal with: maggots and flies, hair and body lice, rats and mice. As eradication was impossible, the soldiers could only do their best to avoid infestations by keeping their environment relatively clean. Another serious problem was 'trench foot'. The footwear of soldiers allowed their feet to get damp and cold for prolonged periods of time. This resulted in swelling and secondary infections, which would lead to painful skin peeling and even loss of toes, rendering combatants unable to fight effectively.

British tommies relaxing and having wounds treated in an underground forward dressing station by the Menin Road in France

The Eastern Front

As the main Allied campaign was at the Western Front during World War I, it is often forgotten that there was also an Eastern Front. This is where the Russians, and their allies, took on the Austro-Hungarian army. Thus, the Central Powers had to fight on two flanks, in an effort to increase their empire both eastward and westward. Needless to say, it meant having to spread their resources with inevitable consequences in the long run.

At that time, Russia was in a state of political unrest and its infrastructure was not geared up to the material demands of war on this unprecedented scale. What it did have, however, was a vast population, so it was able to keep replenishing its battalions with new personnel. Nevertheless, the Russian people soon grew disillusioned by the drain on resources and the enormously high casualty rate. To all intents and purposes, it felt as if the Russian monarchy was treating the war as if it were a giant game of chess, with human cost all part of the game.

Adorned with flowers, a soldier of the Austro-Hungarian army prepares to leave for the Eastern Front

Ultimately, this lack of concern for the common people led to revolution in February 1917. Tsar Nicholas was forced to abdicate and the Communist Bolsheviks took power, under the leadership of Vladimir Lenin. Having a new cause to fight for gave the Russian army a morale boost, putting the enemy forces on the back foot. Then the Communists attempted to cease hostilities with the Central Powers, but this resulted in a large-scale offensive from the enemy, sensing weakness in the Russian resolve.

The Eastern Front finally fell peaceful in March 1918, with the Treaty of Brest-Litovsk. This enabled the Central Powers to divert their spare forces to the Western Front in the hope of finally winning the war. However, it was too late, as the US had declared war on Germany and begun sending troops to France and Belgium, thereby countering the additional manpower.

Unlike the Western Front, the Eastern Front was far more mobile, in both directions, which meant that trench warfare did not typify the theatre of war in that region. This had a good deal to do with the terrain, which was not generally flat and deeply soiled, but far more hilly and mountainous instead. As a result, offensives and counter-offensives moved the frontline considerable distances, as one force advanced and the other retreated.

Action in a British first line trench
in the Balkans, Eastern Front

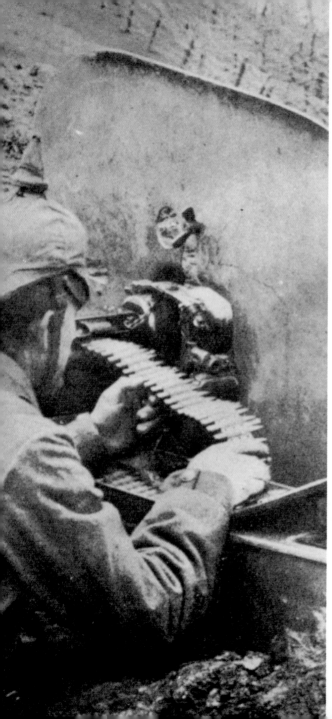

German soldiers operating a
machine gun from a trench
on Russia's Eastern Front

Camouflage

It may be hard to believe, but in the initial stages of World War I, the French wore their traditional blue coats and red trousers on the battlefield. Needless to say, they stood out like sore thumbs against the greens and browns of the countryside and were easily targeted by the German riflemen, artillerymen and particularly the machine gunners. Before too long, the high command admitted that it might be better to give their troops a fighting chance, so they introduced a more neutral coloured uniform in greyish-blue, which was still pretty visible but a marked improvement.

The British had already learnt the value of mimicking the colours of battle terrain in the late 19th century, so they entered the war wearing uniforms in khaki, which is a drab, olive-green colour. Although khaki was a better colour than greyish-blue, both uniforms were still visible to one extent or another, because the background often comprised many hues and tones. Textile technologies were not able to produce the complex patterns needed for more successful camouflage, but this realization led to rapid camouflage developments in other areas on the field of battle.

American soldiers practising with camouflaged artillery after their arrival in France in 1917

A German officer in a
camouflaged position in a
wooded area of the Vosges

Machines of war, such as artillery guns, tanks and troop carriers were soon being painted in contrasting shades and colours, to obscure their outlines and make it more difficult for the enemy to interpret what they were seeing. These developments were accelerated by the introduction of aircraft into the theatre of war. As aircraft were able to view enemy activities from a vantage point, it became increasingly important to hide equipment and personnel. This resulted in the use of camouflaged canvas and netting for the purpose of concealment from above.

As the terrain at the Western Front was typically flat and featureless, it was very obvious if anyone so much as raised their head above the parapet, making reconnaissance rather dangerous. This led to the invention of artificial trees in the hope of gaining an elevated view without being shot. Steel-frame pylons would be hastily erected at night and then camouflaged with bark and foliage to look like shelled stumps. If the enemy had not noticed the change to the scenery the next morning, then it was possible to climb up the pylons and quickly survey the scene in the hope of gaining useful information.

A French soldier in his bright blue uniform, which made them easy targets amongst the green and brown landscapes

Envoi au Front

A la France toujours fidéle,
Sois vigilante sentinelle.

British Soldiers with gun
covered with wheat to hide it
from German aircraft during
World War One Circa 1916

British soldiers moving
forward through wire at the
start of the Battle of the
Somme, 1 July 1916

Machine Guns

To many people, World War I is defined by a number of characteristics that set it apart from wars before and since. In particular, the entrenchment of troops on the Western Front, as both sides found it impossible to launch successful offensives on the flatlands of Belgium and France.

This circumstance arose due to the development of the machine gun and the terrain peculiar to that particular theatre of war. The Germans had a machine gun named the Maschinengewehr 08, which was based on an original design by Hiram Maxim, an American-born, British inventor. He had offered the gun to the British in 1884, but the British high command had not realized its potential. When the war broke out, the Germans already had 12,000 machine guns, and had 100,000 by the close of hostilities.

It is generally agreed that a single machine gun was equivalent to around eighty riflemen, such was its rate of fire. As a consequence, it was virtually impossible to advance across open ground when faced with just one machine gun, let alone several. To make matters worse, the machine

Gas-masked men of the British Machine Gun Corps with a Vickers machine gun during the first battle of the Somme

gun had such a concentration of fire that it was possible to have one's body cleaved in two by the stream of bullets.

Maxim's gun design utilized the exhaust gases of each preceding bullet to provide the energy required to load and fire the following bullet. This is why it was called a machine gun, and it was a simple and efficient design. It would fire at a rate of 300-600 rounds per minute, depending on how well maintained it was in field conditions.

The British, having failed to realize the advantages of the machine gun, had only a handful of old Maxim machine guns in 1914. By 1915, having suffered heavy losses, the British established its Machine Gun Corps using a different design called the Vickers machine gun.

Both the Maschinengewehr 08 and the Vickers were heavy pieces of equipment, requiring a number of personnel to operate them. This meant that they were better used for defensive warfare as they were not easily portable, as would be necessary for offensive operations. Eventually, assault machine guns came into use as the technology was developed sufficiently for lightweight designs. These included the Lewis machine gun, used by the Allies, and the Bergman MP18 sub-machine gun, used by the Germans.

Soldiers of the 16th Canadian machine gun regiment using shell holes as makeshift defences at Passchendaele Ridge

US soldiers of 23rd Infantry, 2nd Div. firing a 37MM infantry
machine gun at a German position

A German machine gun division with six captured Russian guns at Tirlancourt

Shell Shock

In the Edwardian era, psychiatry was very much in its embryonic stage of development. This meant that the psychological symptoms of warfare were not tolerated, simply because they were not understood. These days, many soldiers are diagnosed with Post Traumatic Stress Disorder following combat, because the combination of long periods of anticipation followed by intense action and stress can have damaging effects on the nervous system.

During World War I, increasing numbers of troops began to suffer from nerve related behaviours, ranging from inability to face the enemy, to extreme reactions to noise, characterized by uncontrollable twitching and ticks. This became known as shell shock, and rendered many combatants disabled and unable to continue fighting. Prolonged exposure to the terror of shell fire, along with the sight of others blown to pieces, was too much for many to take, so their nervous systems closed down with alarming results.

In a way, it was better for those who displayed physical symptoms, as they were taken away to hospital for treatment, in the hope that rest and quiet might cure them of their afflictions. Those who developed lesser symptoms would often disobey orders or even run away to avoid subjecting themselves to further panic. This was interpreted as cowardice by commanding officers, who frequently had no first-hand experience of the horrors of frontline conditions. As a result, many were imprisoned and even shot as an example to others. Had the establishment had a better understanding of psychiatry, then they would have realized that these behaviours were involuntary.

Soldiers suffering from shell
shock take up gardening to help
them recover

71

War in the Air

As World War I began just ten years after the first flight of a powered aeroplane, it may seem remarkable that they were developed sufficiently to be useful machines in the theatre of war. However, their evolution had been rapid, because they captured the public imagination. Aviators were frequently setting themselves new challenges to see what their flying machines could do, and this resulted in accelerated progress. By the time the war had started, the aeroplane was reliable and had begun to take on the fundamental form upon which modern machines are typically designed.

Initially, aeroplanes were put to use for the purpose of reconnaissance over land and sea. As the Western Front was situated on such flat terrain it was virtually impossible to gain a vantage point without being shot. The aeroplane had the advantage of being able to fly out of gun range and above enemy-held territory, so that it was possible to take photographs of enemy positions.

English SE-5 single-seater plane (top) and a German Rumpler two-seater in aerial combat on the British front

Needless to say, both sides had the same idea, so
the aeroplane quickly adapted from an observation
device to a machine of war, able to attack other
aircraft and defend itself from their attentions too.

Many biplane and monoplane designs appeared,
as engineers tried to keep their machines ahead
in the arms race. Having machine guns became a
vital component of these warplanes, but propellers
presented an obstacle to the passage of bullets.
Some designs had twin engines, to allow the guns
to be mounted in between.

Some had pushing propellers, to allow the guns to
sit in front. Others had rear-mounted gunners to
defend against attack from the rear. Eventually, a
mechanism was invented to allow the machine
gun to fire through the rotating propeller blades,
which meant that dog-fights became a feature of
airborne warfare.

A common problem with these early aeroplanes was that they had very little payload. They were simply not powerful and fast enough to lift much additional weight off the ground. This meant there was no possibility of carrying armour plating, so aircrew were always vulnerable to being hit by bullets from other aeroplanes and from the ground.

It also meant that the concept of the aeroplane as a bomber was only in its infancy when the World War I ended. The concept of the fighter, however, was well and truly established.

Before the Royal Air Force existed in Britain, military airmen either belonged to the Royal Flying Corps, as part of the British Army, or the Royal Naval Air Service, as part of the Royal Navy. By April 1918, the potential of military aircraft had been fully accepted and both forces merged to create the RAF.

British SE-5s locked in aerial
combat, or dogfight, with
German Fokker D7s

German flying ace Heinrich
Gontermann stands near his
Fokker DR-1 tri-plane on an
airfield, Germany

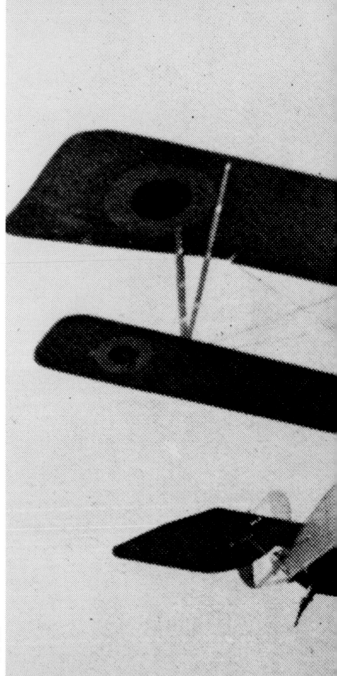

A French-built
Nieuport XXIII
reconnaissance
plane, circa 1916

Battles of Ypres

Many battles at the Western Front during World War I were centred around a strategically important town named Ypres, in West Flanders, which is a municipality of Belgium. During the course of the war, many offensives and defensives were fought along a frontline running roughly north-south. Although their exact positions varied, many came to be known as the Battles of Ypres.

The first Battle of Ypres, in the autumn of 1914, established the pattern of trench warfare that would become synonymous with World War I. This was the result of some key factors. For one thing, many trained, regular soldiers perished in the hail of machine gun fire, so that they were replaced by volunteers. Also, reconnaissance information was lacking, which led to indecisive campaigns based largely on guesswork. As a consequence, both the Allies and the Germans found themselves losing personnel as quickly as they could be transported to the front, and a stalemate situation resulted.

In their individual shelters, on the front line, British soldiers, bayonet attached to their rifle barrel, await the German attack during the Battle of Ypres

Worst of all though, was the way in which the military was structured. The high command did not play an active role in the field. As a result, they kept sending lines of soldiers across no-man's-land, without appreciating that they were so easily cut down by enemy machine guns. Even though they were aware of such dreadfully high casualty rates, this lack of first-hand experience meant that it simply didn't impact them sufficiently to implement different tactics. The phrase 'going over the top' became part of the battlefield vernacular, as it was the command feared the most by the ordinary soldier, knowing it meant almost certain death. It also meant a pointless death, as it served no strategic purpose whatsoever.

Hundreds of thousands of Allies and Germans became casualties of war in Flanders, either killed, injured or missing in action. The exact numbers are not known, because records are imprecise. Astonishingly, nearly fifty thousand went missing during the Battles of Ypres. This is largely because they fell in no-man's-land and it was impossible to retrieve their corpses. Over time, shellfire either buried them or blew them to pieces, until there was no evidence of their having been there in the first place.

The endemic problem with the military high command's inability to empathize with the common man, was a result of the class structure in general society. Just as the Black Death caused a societal shift away from feudalism, due to the resulting lack of available manpower, so World War I would cause a similar societal shift away from the Victorian master-servant set-up. So, it can at least be said that the legacy of those who so needlessly died, was the initiation of a better society.

British Soldiers in the Trenches
during the Battle of Ypres in
Belgium circa 1917

Stretcher bearers struggle
in mud up to their knees
to carry a wounded
man to safety during
the third battle of Ypres
(Passchendaele)

Belgian soldiers rush to
commence battle, on the
banks of a canal near Ypres

War at Sea

During World War I, warfare at sea played a significant factor, because it was all about supply of personnel and materials to and from other regions of the world. The Allies and the Central Powers both had substantial naval forces with which to do battle, but the Germans had developed the U-boat, which proved to be a particularly effective weapon against military vessels, merchant ships and troop carriers.

The U-boat (Underwater boat) was a class of submarine especially developed by the Germans for covert operations, able to fire torpedoes at the hulls of these craft with an element of surprise and devastation, which the Allies found difficult to counter. Sonar was yet to be invented and the British experimented with hydrophones in an effort to detect the engine noises of approaching U-boats with little success.

A British steamer is torpedoed.
The picture was taken from
the German U-Boat which
made the attack

The role of the reconnaissance aeroplane became important as it was one of the best ways of detecting U-boats. It was then possible to alert shipping of their presence. The only effective way to counter-attack U-boats was to drop depth charges and hope that the pressure waves would damage them sufficiently to either sink them or force them to the surface. For the most part though, it was better for cargo ships to travel in convoys, protected by military escorts. Until the introduction of escorts, U-boats had a field day sinking hundreds of supply ships bound for Britain and France from the US.

Eventually the U-boats were rendered unable to sink sufficient numbers of Allied transport ships to have any serious effect on the supply chain to the frontline. The actions of U-boats against US ships also prompted the Americans to declare war on Germany, so the outcome of the war became inevitable.

As the U-boats are so well documented in history, it is often forgotten that the British had a number of World War I submarines of their own. They were primarily used in an effort to counter the U-boat threat, albeit with only limited success. The most numerous design was the E-class, of which 58 were launched between 1912 and 1916. They were also used to lay mines across shipping lanes used by the enemy and to assist in campaigns where troops needed to be delivered to coastal regions.

The interior of a British E-class submarine, 1916

A U-boat opens fire with a deck cannon, on an allied merchant ship

Tanks

The Battle of the Somme was the first battle in which a tank was used. The stalemate situation of trench warfare had arisen due to a peculiar combination of traditional tactics and advancing technology, which meant neither side was able to move forward in any decisive way. The idea behind the tank was simply a means of traversing the battlefield without being mown down by machine gun fire. It was a case of necessity being the mother of invention.

The first tanks were, however, only prototypes, as the Battle of the Somme was effectively their testing ground. They were unwieldy and unreliable, so that operators found them difficult to manoeuvre - especially under heavy fire - and would often find themselves stranded in no-man's-land, unable to restart their engines. In addition, they had poor visibility and limited effectiveness in terms of their own ability to return fire. This was because they had not yet adopted the standard tank format, with a rotating turret mounted above the traction unit. Instead, they had guns mounted to the side, between the track rails.

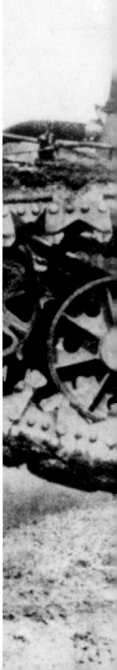

First World War tanks were descendants of vehicles like this early caterpillar-track farm machine

The German A7V tank, created by
Daimler-Benz, weighed 26 tons and
had a top speed of 12km/h; it carried a
crew of up to 18 men

In short, tanks were primitive and poorly designed. As a concept though, their potential was clear enough, as they did indeed protect their occupants and they protected troops who used them as moving shields. In addition, they had a significant psychological effect on the enemy, who feared being crushed to death by the cumbersome machines as they trundled blindly over trenches and dug-outs.

The idea of the tank came from a British soldier named Ernest Dunlop Swinton. A friend had mentioned that an armoured tractor might be useful at the front, so Swinton began to think about ways of combining the basic concept of the track-propelled tractor, which had only just been invented, with a capacity to carry artillery.

The name 'tank' came about simply because the first machines were nothing more than mobile metal tanks. This early format, without the familiar gun turret, arose because the available technology was limited and it made sense to have everything contained within a single chamber and with a low centre of gravity.

By the close of World War I, the tank had begun to evolve rapidly. Ironically, it was the Germans who recognized its true potential and subsequently perfected its design between the wars. In 1940 the Panzer tanks used by the Germans, in their Blitzkrieg of Western Europe, were state-of-the-art machines that destroyed the tanks available to the Allies.

An American soldier walks ahead of an MKIV British-made tank, 1918

British tanks in action with German
shells bursting around them, 1917

Zeppelins

R igid airships, or dirigibles, were conceived in the late 19th century and the first flight took place in 1900, preceding the first powered aeroplane flight by three years. The name Zeppelin became synonymous with airships because it was the German pioneer Count Ferdinand von Zeppelin who got the idea off the ground, quite literally. Unlike hot air balloons, which relied on hot air being less dense than cold air, Zeppelins relied on the relative density of gases. They were filled with the lightweight gas hydrogen, which was less dense than the combination of gases in the atmosphere.

As Zeppelins could be made very large, it meant that they could carry considerable payloads, making them perfect for transporting passengers and their luggage. They could also be propelled with engines and piloted, again unlike hot air balloons, so that regular services were established. Inevitably, the German military saw great potential in Zeppelins when World War I broke out. Zeppelins were ideal for scouting missions and for bombing the enemy.

The Army airship Beta II at Aldershot, 1915

Mays', Aldershot,

Wrecked houses at St.
Peter's Plain, Yarmouth
after a Zeppelin bombing
raid, January 1915

A newspaper vendor in a London
street announces the news of a
Zeppelin raid on England

They had a few drawbacks, as they were ill-suited
to operating in windy weather conditions and
hydrogen is highly flammable, taking only a spark
to set it alight, but aeroplanes were simply not
advanced enough to do a better job at that stage
in history. So, Zeppelins were used extensively by
the Germans, especially in situations that required
prolonged reconnaissance work, such as detecting
warships in the Baltic and North Sea. Aeroplanes
simply did not have the range or fuel capacity to
remain airborne for long enough.

Zeppelins were even used for bombing raids over
Britain, which came as quite a shock in a world
coming to terms with the possibilities of flight
in general. A number of east coast towns, cities
and docks were targeted with success, not least
because Britain was yet to implement a strategy
against air raids. By 1916 many anti-aircraft
guns and searchlights were positioned on British
territory to counter the Zeppelin threat. In truth,
the bombing raids did relatively little damage in
material terms, but their psychological effect was
considerable as no one had imagined that they
might be in danger in their own homes when the
frontline was hundreds of miles away in France.

This also called into question whether it was ethically acceptable to bomb civilians. Inevitably, British sentiment towards the Germans grew increasingly negative. Kaiser Wilhelm did initially order that primary targets should be places of strategic value and that bombing in an indiscriminate manner simply to terrorize was to be avoided. As the war progressed however, such considerations went out the window, and Zeppelins increasingly dropped bombs and incendiaries where they could. City defences improved however, so the airships began to target less densely populated places.

A German L21 Zeppelin sinks off the coast of Yarmouth, Norfolk, after having been shot down

Artillery

Trench warfare made rifles, pistols and machine guns relatively ineffective at reaching the enemy, unless they happened to attempt an assault or were foolish enough to expose themselves to gunfire. This meant that other field weapons were increasingly relied upon to strike at the unseen enemy. These weapons characteristically had parabolic trajectories so that the projectile came down from above and hopefully fell into enemy trenches.

The handheld grenade was designed for this very purpose, as it could be thrown in an arc, but it required the soldier to be near enough for the grenade to reach the target. This was virtually impossible as the soldier would need to leave his own trench and traverse no-man's-land to be within range. As a result, the mortar was developed, which was basically a mechanically assisted grenade. It was ejected from a launch tube and was capable of travelling several hundred yards.

Belgian gun crew at work during the Siege of Antwerp, 1914

Three 8-inch Howitzers of 39th
Siege Battery, Royal Garrison
Artillery (RGA), firing from the
Fricourt-Mametz Valley during
the Battle of the Somme

123

Next on the scale were the field guns. They were capable of firing exploding shells over several miles distance, so they were stationed a long way behind the frontline in order that their ammunition fell on the enemy at the correct angle to do maximum damage. Needless to say, the room for error was considerable, so accurate sighting adjustments relied greatly on reconnaissance information. Even then, the targeting could be quite arbitrary, so the big guns kept firing until they had given the whole area a good pounding. Of course, it was also possible to be hit by friendly fire, if the artillerymen set their guns with too short a range.

The most frequently used artillery were Howitzers. They were short barrelled guns that fell somewhere between mortars and field guns in terms of their firepower and their trajectory. They were also relatively lightweight and mobile, making them ideally suited to being moved about behind the field of battle. As Howitzers were designed to fire ammunition over relatively short distances, at high trajectories, they were capable of delivering shells twice the size of those delivered by equivalent field guns.

Captured German 21cm howitzers, WW1

The combination of the steep angle of attack and large shell size made them formidable weapons when they hit target. If a battery of Howitzers launched a simultaneous attack, then whole areas containing enemy positions could be obliterated in minutes. The aim was to breach the enemy's frontline in this way, so that offensives could quickly be launched before the enemy had time to recover and defend themselves. This usually worked for only short periods of time, so that the Western Front changed shape here and there, but essentially remained in the same place year after year.

German 21cm howitzers preparing
to retire, WW1

Belgian soldiers make a charge near the River Yser

British troops hauling a gun
into position under cover of a
ridge at Salonika

131

Chemical Warfare

O nce the Allies and the Central Powers had settled into trench warfare on the Western Front, it marked a sea-change in the strategic psychology of those orchestrating the warfare. Realizing that conventional weapons were failing to break the deadlock, they got to thinking about new technologies that might make a difference. This led to the unfortunate use of gaseous chemicals in efforts to incapacitate large numbers of the enemy while they languished in their trenches, foxholes and dug-outs.

The first gas to be used in this way was chlorine. The Germans used it against the Allies at the Second Battle of Ypres in 1915 and the British were quick to retaliate. However, the dispersal of gas requires a favourable wind and the British ended up gassing their own troops. Chlorine is an extreme irritant when inhaled, because it reacts chemically with water to produce hydrochloric acid and

Two US soldiers wear gas masks while walking through plumes of smoke, 1917

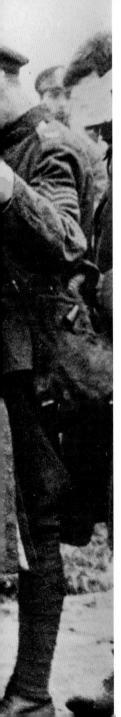

hypochlorous acid. Relatively few victims of chlorine gas died, but they were rendered unable to fight for considerable periods of time. In addition, chlorine gas was visible and odorous, so that it had a detrimental psychological effect on soldiers when they realized a cloud of the gas was coming their way. As it was heavier than air, it would creep along the ground and pool into low-lying places, forcing troops to evacuate their hiding places and expose themselves to enemy fire.

The second gas to be used in World War I was phosgene, which is a compound of chlorine with oxygen and carbon. Unlike chlorine, phosgene was invisible and virtually odourless, making it more effective at poisoning the enemy, because they found it more difficult to detect. Its effects were more lethal too, although it took some time before the necessary chemical reactions had taken place. The phosgene molecules prevented the lungs from absorbing oxygen, so the victim died from asphyxia.

British casualties blinded by mustard gas in a German gas attack at Bethune, France

Gassed and blinded French infantrymen are led by comrades, and escorted
by British soldiers from the second Battle of the Marne

The third gas was mustard gas, which was also a compound of chlorine, with sulphur, carbon and hydrogen. Mustard gas killed far fewer soldiers than phosgene, but it became far more notorious due to the unsightly and painful blistering it caused on contact with the skin and airways. Mustard gas was used extensively by the Central Powers against the Russians on the Eastern Front.

Various gas masks with chemical filters were developed to counter the effects of these gases, but mustard gas proved more difficult to deal with due to its vesicant properties, which rendered soldiers inoperative even if they managed to avoid inhaling it or being blinded by it.

French troops wearing an early form of gas mask in the trenches during the 2nd Battle of Ypres

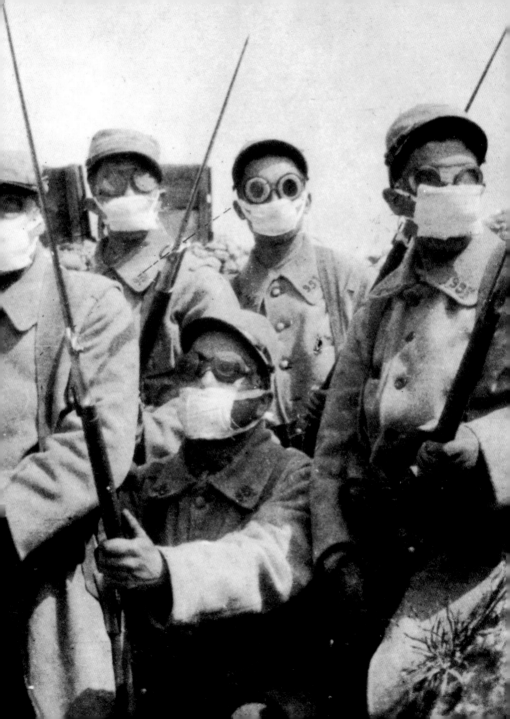

Flamethrowers

O ne of the drawbacks with using chemical weapons at the Western Front was that the lingering gases would often make it hazardous for troops to advance, even if their gas attacks had been successful. As a result, military engineers were tasked with devising other ways of flushing the enemy from their trenches. This led to the development of the flamethrower. It was essentially nothing more than a stream of burning flammable liquid pumped under high pressure towards the target.

In places where the enemy was close by, the flamethrower proved quite effective at filling trenches with flames so that the occupants had no option but to evacuate into the line of fire of rifles and machine guns. Incredibly, in some parts of the frontline opposing trenches were fewer than five metres apart, but typically they were separated by a swathe of no-man's-land measuring more than fifty metres.

Austrian soldiers on the
Eastern Front preparing to
throw burning liquids

One of the first flamethrowers used by the
French against an enemy trench

This presented a problem for flamethrowers, because they were not yet portable, so their range was limited by the distance the fuel could be thrown. As a result, engineers dug tunnels beneath no-man's-land so that it was possible to emerge closer to the enemy and surprise them with a shower of flames.

The Germans made extensive use of semi-portable flamethrowers during World War I, as they were effective at intimidating the enemy and so preventing them from advancing. The most ambitious flamethrowers were built by the British.

They were called Livens Flame Projectors and were so big that their use was only intended to be part of the shock tactics in launching effective offensives. Five are known to have been made, but only three were put to use.

Two saw action in the Battle of the Somme, sending enormous jets of flame from no-man's-land prior to troop advances. They probably achieved little in terms of actually killing the enemy, but they certainly struck fear into the hearts of the Germans, for it is known that fewer Allies perished at the points where the flamethrowers were deployed.

The designer, William Livens, also engineered a wide-bore mortar, called the Livens Projector. It was used to fire large canister bombs containing flammable liquids and toxic chemicals over distances of several hundred yards. Intriguingly, the canister bombs were sometimes filled with malodorous but harmless substances, to trick the enemy into thinking they were being exposed to harmful gases.

The bodies of hundreds of Italian
soldiers lie dead on the battlefield,
victims of flame attack

A British tank burns furiously, having been caught in the jet of a
flamethrower and its fuel contents ignited

Gallipoli Campaign

With Russia as part of the Entente, along with Britain and France, it was in the Allies' interests to have a sea route from the Mediterranean to Russia. This meant having to secure part of the Ottoman Empire, so that safe passage could be made through the Sea of Marmara to the Black Sea, via the Bosphorus.

Dreadnoughts bombard the
heights of Chocolate Hill
and Lalu Baba and cover
our advance from Suvla Bay,
Gallipoli, Turkey

In order to achieve this, a force was sent to seize the Gallipoli peninsula, so that the Dardanelles strait would be under Allied control. Then, the Allied force would continue eastward to take the city of Constantinople (Istanbul), thereby completing the objective. At least, that was the plan. As it turned out, things went disastrously wrong.

Due to Allied commitments at the Western Front, only a small naval expeditionary force was dispatched to invade the peninsula. The terrain was difficult and led to an initial withdrawal. By the time a larger force arrived, the element of surprise had been wasted and the Turks had amassed a considerable force ready to defend their territory. As a result, the Allies found themselves pinned along the coast with the Turks holding the higher ground inland. Both sides continued feeding in reinforcements, but the frontline remained more-or-less frozen.

After nine months of ferocious hostilities, the Allies finally decided to cut their losses in December 1915, and withdraw. They had lost over 70,000 men, while the Turks had lost about 60,000. It was one of the most costly campaigns of World War I and achieved nothing except to highlight just how wasteful modern warfare could be.

Over 11,000 of the Allied losses were ANZAC
(Australian and New Zealand Army Corp).
They had travelled half way around the world,
only to be slaughtered.

Weather conditions on the Gallipoli peninsula
made life particularly difficult for the Allies.
In the summer it grew unbearably hot, so that
corpses decomposed very rapidly and the smell of
putrefying flesh filled the air. In the winter it grew
unbearably cold, with flash floods filling trenches
and drowning troops. The general lack of hygiene
also resulted in outbreaks of dysentery. With no
prospect of a successful outcome to the campaign,
morale fell so low that evacuation was the only
option left available.

Turkish troops on parade at
Gallipoli, 1915

The Battle of the Somme

The Somme is a river in north-eastern France, just south of Flanders in Belgium. The word 'somme' is derived from the Celtic for tranquillity, which is about as ironic as anything can possibly be. Ironic, because in terms of human loss of life, the Battle of the Somme was one of the most costly of all time, with over a million killed between 1st July and 18th November 1916. The banks of the Somme were anything but tranquil for those tragic weeks and the battle changed the public perception of war forever, because so many families were affected in such a short space of time.

The original intention behind the offensive that marked the beginning of the Battle of the Somme, was for the Allies to punch a hole through the German frontline and attempt to bring the war to a conclusion. However, the Germans proved to be a formidable enemy and prevented a breach from occurring. The battle then developed into a slanging match of countless attacks and counter-attacks, so that fighting became contained within a particular area only a few miles wide and about fifteen miles long.

Canadian troops prepare for the charge over the top at the Battle of the Somme, 1916

Although the Somme frontline moved
insufficiently to justify the vast numbers of
casualties, it is now considered to have been a
pivotal battle in World War I, because attrition to
the German army was considerable and led to a
retreat a couple of months later to the Hindenburg
line, some forty miles east. Whereas the Allies
were able to reinforce their forces following the
battle, the Germans were not, so they had suffered
a damaging blow.

The tragedy is that it took so many lives, on both
sides, to achieve the necessary bias in strength
for the Allies to get the upper hand. The same
result could have been achieved by sending the
million soldiers home to their families, but that
is where World War I differed from past conflicts.
Traditionally, armies were more representative
of populations rather than comprising such a high
percentage of the populations themselves. As a
consequence, battles were fought more like games
of chess, in a chosen location on a certain day, to
determine the winner. As a result, relatively few
lost their lives to the ritual. Modern warfare had
become an unnecessary cull of those who were
needed to maintain the infrastructure of society
when hostilities ceased.

A German soldier wearing a gas
mask about to hurl a hand-grenade
from a trench during The Battle of
the Somme

Roll call of the 1st Battalion, Lancashire
Fusiliers on the afternoon of 1 July 1916,
following their assault on Beaumont
Hamel, Battle of the Somme

163

Canadian troops with fixed
bayonets leaving their
trenches for a raid
on the Somme

War-horses,
War-dogs
and War-pigeons

French Lancers on horseback
follow up a German retreat

British soldiers in the south of England train a carrier pigeon to deliver messages during World War I

Perhaps due to the enormous human cost of World War I, it is often forgotten that many animals died in the conflict too. Of course, large areas of natural habitat were turned to fields of mud and laced with poisonous chemicals, so many wild animals would have perished as a result, but here we consider the domesticated animals used by the armed forces in the war effort.

It is reckoned that about half a million war-horses died in the service of both the Allies and the Central Powers. As tracked vehicles, such as tanks and gun tractors, were only introduced and developed during the war, it meant that horses were still the best way of carrying and pulling equipment over uneven terrain. They were also very effective transportation for personnel, either on horseback, as cavalry, on in troop wagons. Horses therefore played an important role at the Western Front while the front lines were fluid and mobile.

When the trench warfare began, horses took a supporting role, working between the supply heads and the back trenches, to ensure that ammunition, foodstuffs and other provisions found their way to those who needed them.

On the Eastern Front, where entrenchment was less frequent, horses continued to play a central role in the military movements of the Russians and the Austro-Hungarians. It should be remembered also, that there were few roads in Eastern Europe, so the horse was a vital mode of transport and traction over rough country.

Incredibly, about a million war-dogs lost their lives in World War I. They were used to carry messages at the Western Front, and in other frontline zones, where it was too dangerous for humans to risk exposing themselves. Portable radio systems were not yet available, so a physical means of delivering messages was essential. As a result, the dogs were actively targeted by the enemy to prevent the communications from reaching their intended destinations. Messages would be inserted in canisters secured to the dogs' collars.

For long-distance communications, thousands of war-pigeons were used. Having been kept in pigeon lofts at headquarters, they would use their homing instincts to return to those lofts when released in the field. Messages would be inserted into tubes attached to the pigeons' legs. As pigeons are quite swift flyers they stood a reasonable chance of returning without being shot from the skies. Many British homing pigeons flew from Belgium and France to England. It became illegal to shoot pigeons for sport or food, in case they happened to be winged messengers. Also, many peregrine falcons were shot to prevent them from hunting the pigeons en route.

French troops with dogs, 1916

Hindenburg Line

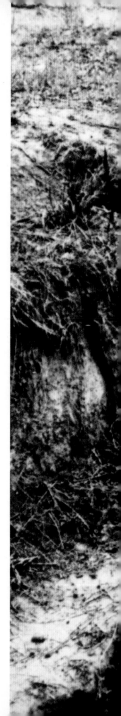

Known at the time as the Siegfried Line, but now known as the Hindenburg Line, to avoid confusion with a similar boundary in World War II, it was a fortified line of retreat prepared by the Germans as a precautionary measure, just in case they found themselves in a situation where they needed to lick their wounds. As it turned out, the Battle of the Somme depleted the Germans so much that they had no choice but to give up a forty mile swathe of territory in order to fall back.

The Hindenburg Line was a string of fortifications and tank barriers, designed to keep the Allies at bay while the Germans regrouped and replenished their forces. The Germans had a shortage of manpower because they were fighting on two fronts and this is what compromised them into retreat. Added to this, they had problems with the supply of equipment and munitions.

A section of a Hindenburg trench near Cologne Farm

British and French troops in reserve lines at Le Verquier, 25 April 1917, following the German retreat to the Hindenburg Line.

Many soldiers with engineering skills were returned to the German industrial regions in an effort to improve production. In the meantime, the remaining German army had to defend the Hindenburg Line until the situation improved.

The British had, themselves, experienced a shortage of shells known as the Shell Crisis in 1915, which resulted in political reforms to ensure that the entire British economy was geared towards the war effort. New factories were built and labour forces recruited to manufacture adequate numbers of shells and the materials needed.

Eventually the fortunes of the Germans seemed to be improving when Eastern Front hostilities died away due to civil unrest within Russia. The Communists took control in 1917 and it wasn't in their interests to continue fighting the war, because they had their own civil war to deal with.

This meant that the Central Powers found themselves able to redeploy redundant forces along the Western Front and once again push westward away from the Hindenburg Line.

However, the Germans had provoked the USA into declaring war by sinking RMS Lusitania in 1915 and US troops had begun pouring into Europe, ready to join the war effort. As a result, the Germans simply could not muster sufficient resources to counter the influx of Allied troops.

The writing was on the wall for the Germans and the Hindenburg Line came to represent their Achilles' heel during the interwar years. That is why crossing the Hindenburg Line became so symbolic for Adolf Hitler during his invasion of Western Europe
in 1940.

Wounded Canadian soldiers
within the Hindenburg Line
are being taken back from
the firing lines by captured
German prisoners

Frontline Defences

As the Western Front descended into trench warfare, it became necessary to put up defences as protection from enemy fire and from enemy encroachment. The trenches were a form of defence in themselves, of course, as they provided places for soldiers to conceal themselves. In addition, the soil dug out to form the trenches was used to create bunds in front of the trenches. These would absorb enemy fire and provide additional height for the protection of soldiers.

No-man's-land, the zone between opposed trenches, was another matter. It was desirable to install barricades to prevent the enemy from launching raids, but it was also necessary to be able to see what was going on. This is where barbed wire came into its own. Coils of barbed wire presented a formidable obstacle to would-be raiders, yet it was easy to see through and it had the added advantage of being virtually impossible to breach with grenades and machine gun fire. It was also lightweight and inexpensive.

German troops arranging barbed wire defences to their trench, 1916

Many Allies and enemy found themselves entangled on barbed wire, which more often than not, meant death from gunfire. It was possible to pass under or through it, but not in a hurry. In fact, the more soldiers struggled the more entwined they became and the more hopeless their prospects became too.

When the tank was introduced, however, barbed wire immediately had its limitations. Tanks would roll straight over it and allow pursuing combatants to run across unhindered. Thus the tank changed the rules, so that barbed wire became largely redundant, except in places where tanks could not manage the terrain.

A device called a Bangalore torpedo was invented for the purpose of breaching barbed wire obstacles. It comprised a number of articulated tubes so that, when explosively fired, it would unravel and sweep the barbed wire away. Of course, wire cutters were also available but there was a high risk of being shot whilst attempting to sever the wires. Also, the Germans introduced an extra thick wire, which proved impossible to cut by hand.

Allied soldier as he stands with fixed bayonet across no-man's-land amid barbed wire obstacles during a battle on the Western Front

German sniper, lying on the ground behind barbed
wire entanglements, 1918

The combination of barbed wire and machine guns
maintained the stalemate on the Western Front
for a considerable period of time. Neither side was
able to mobilize for exactly the same reasons, so
the war became a process of attrition. Hundreds of
thousands died on an un-altering stage, because
the theatre of war was unable to travel.

Balloons

When the Western Front had settled into trench warfare, the most immediate problem was acquiring intelligence about what the enemy was up to. For the Germans, this wasn't such a problem, because they had established their positions on what little high ground there was available. These hills were not large, but they gave the Germans a considerable advantage when all around was so flat, as they could observe the Allies.

Aeroplanes were used to make reconnaissance flyovers, but there was always the risk of having them shot from the air and they were expensive to keep in the air for long periods of time. For this reason, balloons were developed by the Allies and the Germans, to enable prolonged observation of activities across no man's land.

These observation balloons were filled with either hydrogen or coal gas (a gas mixture) to make them lighter than air. They had to be tethered to the ground by ropes or cables to prevent them from blowing away with the wind, so they were kept well behind the frontline, out of the range of enemy fire. Observers were suspended from baskets below the balloons and communicated with the ground via telephone lines, which hung down.

A German observation balloon is filled with gas, 1915

A number of balloon designs were developed to provide stability for the observers, so that they weren't forever spinning and changing direction. The Allies favoured the kite balloon, while the Germans favoured the drachen (dragon) balloon. Both had a front end and a tail, so that they would sit still with the prevailing wind and allow the observers to do their job. In order to keep them taut on their guy-wires, the balloons were fitted with pockets to catch the breeze, in a similar way to the sails on a yacht.

On a good day, with sufficient altitude and clear conditions, observers could see usefully for twenty or thirty miles, which was especially useful for instructing artillery batteries in adjusting their howitzers and field guns.

The launch of a hot-air
balloon used for reconnaissance, 1915

Due to the risk of being hit by artillery shells, the balloon operators were the first to make routine use of parachutes. The packed parachute had not been invented, so aeroplane crews had no means of escape, but observation balloons had hung parachutes, ready for immediate use.

Barrage balloons were also devised during World War I, but they were not used in theatres of battle. Instead, they were used in cities in an effort to prevent aircraft from making bombing raids. They were unmanned balloons that carried cables to deter aircraft, but they were only effective at relatively low altitudes, because the cables were heavy to lift.

Austrian soldiers in Albania, filling a balloon with gas

Trench Design

In typical warfare, trenches are temporary structures, occupied for a few hours or a few days at most. On the Western Front, the situation was entirely different, as trenches were occupied for weeks, months or even years. As a result, their design was rather more considered, from a number of viewpoints. From an offensive point of view, trenches needed to provide soldiers with places to fire weapons and points where it was possible to leave the front of the trench to mount assaults across no-man's-land. From a defensive point of view, trenches needed to protect soldiers from enemy gun and shell fire, and make it difficult for raiding parties to mount effective attacks.

Long-term trenches also needed to be stable, to ensure that the sides didn't collapse. They also needed to include billets, where soldiers could eat and sleep when off-duty. In addition, there was the matter of ablutions and sanitation. In other words, trenches needed to cater for day-to-day requirements of their human occupants over long periods of time.

An American sniper in France hiding behind barricades, 1918

A trench in the low flat country
near La Bassee Villa, 1917

Trenches were usually equipped with duck-boarding on the ground, to provide an even and dry surface for the soldiers' feet. Wooden shuttering was also used on the sides of trenches to provide stability, and to form the walls and roofs of dug-outs and toilets. Frontline trenches would often include alcoves and bends, so that raiders were unable to simply jump in one end and fire their guns along the entirety of the trench and kill the occupants.

Many trenches were designed as a system, to allow the rotation of personnel. A central gallery trench, running towards the frontline, would have perpendicular trenches radiating outwards on either side. Typically, there would be frontline trenches, support-line trenches and reserve-line trenches, so that a community of soldiers would take it in turns to carry out different duties. The central gallery trench was heavily defended, because it was the conduit between all other trenches.

All-in-all, life in the trenches was pretty
miserable. As well as the constant threat of death,
conditions were perpetually dirty and unhygienic,
so it was essential that soldiers were given time
away from the frontline, to raise their spirits
and lift their morale. A number of entertainment
troupes were sent to the Western Front for this
purpose. They would put on amusing shows to
encourage troops to laugh, relax and socialize.
Having their minds distracted from the daily
horrors of warfare was considered to be
vital therapy.

A deserted trench in Ypres,
Belgium, site of three World
War I battles

Medicine

Disease and infection were responsible for more death in World War I than any other cause. Squalid, insanitary conditions on the Western Front, the Eastern Front and the Ottoman Front made the likelihood of contracting ailments very high.

Antibiotics had not been discovered, so bacterial infections were a serious problem. Communicable bacterial illnesses, such as tuberculosis, dysentery, typhus and cholera would spread rapidly due to a general lack of hygiene and the close proximity of the combatants. Similarly all battle wounds, large and small, had the potential to become infected, simply because the environment was filled with bacteria.

Three German soldiers display rats killed in their trench the previous night, 1916

Pieces of rotting cadaver and faeces littered the earth surrounding the trenches. In addition, there were pests, such as rats, flies, fleas and lice, which carried bacteria around with them.

Many injuries became gangrenous with bacterial infection. The flesh dies (necrosis), leading to blood poisoning (septicaemia) and then death. Without antibiotics, the only available treatment was to cut the dead tissue away or amputate limbs so that the remaining flesh was free of infection and stood a reasonable chance of healing. Of course, the success of this surgery in turn relied on keeping the newly exposed tissue free from further infection, with the use of disinfectants and dressings. In the field, this was by no means easy to achieve.

Surviving combat injuries was very much a matter of the nature of the injury and its location on the body. Head and body injuries were far more likely to end in death than injuries to the arms and legs. Also, shrapnel injuries tended to be worse than bullet injuries, because the fragments of shell would rip through the flesh, causing considerable damage. Dirty debris would also be introduced to the body, because shells exploded on contact with the ground. Penetrating injuries were always difficult because of the difficulty in removing the foreign bodies and then ensuring that the wound was sterile.

Helping a wounded English
soldier on the front in 1915

When daily hostilities ceased, stretchers would be used to carry the injured away from the battlefield. The stretcher bearers would be protected from enemy fire by wearing the Red Cross symbol, which was recognized and respected as a sign of benevolence. The injured would then be taken on to field hospitals, which were large tents filled with beds. If their injuries were minor, then they would be treated and sent back to the front as soon as possible. If their injuries were more serious, then they would be treated and then sent to proper hospitals further afield, so that the field hospitals had available beds for new casualties.

A wounded soldier has a bandage wrapped around his face as he receives first aid treatment, 1918

An Australian soldier
carries a wounded
comrade to a hospital
during the Dardanelles
Campaign, 1915

Keeping Human

Vital to maintaining the sanity of World War I combatants, whether on land, at sea or in the air, were the small things that meant so much. The postal service was an essential part of the war effort as it allowed loved ones to stay in touch by letter when they were parted for long periods of time and there was a good chance they would never meet again. Much of what historians now know about the human side of the war comes from the letters sent during those years. Most surviving soldiers either chose not to discuss the war, or simply were unable to because it was too emotive. The things they had witnessed were best forgotten for the sake of pursuing a happier life, so the way they achieved this was by trying not to think about it. Over time, they put distance between themselves and their memories. Only in old age, did they feel ready to recount their experiences, motivated by their desire to make sure the world did not forget the enormous sacrifice.

British soldiers eating hot rations in the Ancre Valley during the Battle of the Somme, October 1916

Officers versus other ranks in a football match played by members of the 26th Divisional Ammunition Train near their camp, just outside the city of Salonika, Christmas Day, 25 December 1915

In order to while away the time in between periods of action, men would play card and board games. Nearly everyone smoked in those days, so any form of tobacco was highly valued. Regular soldiers were given a two ounce ration of tobacco per week on the Western Front. Other rations included corned or bully beef, bacon, cheese, sugar, tea, jam, bread, biscuits, condiments, vegetables and rum. Germans rations were much the same, although they included cigars, coffee and snuff.

Frontline British soldiers would also receive a basic pay of one shilling per day. This was used to pay for additional items beyond their rations, such as cigarettes, confectionery, beer and spirits when on short-leave. As an indication of how regular soldiers were regarded by the military high command, those working behind the frontline, running supplies and so on, would receive six times as much, even though their jobs were far less dangerous. It seems that the thinking behind this was; that soldiers seldom had a chance to spend their money anyway, so there was no point in giving them very much. Also, there was a good chance that their cash might be lost on the battlefield, so it wouldn't be circulated back into the war coffers. Fundamentally though, regular soldiers were unskilled and working class, so they stood on the bottom rung of the social ladder, despite putting their necks on the line for the nation.

A female Salvation Army worker writes a letter home for a wounded soldier, 1918

German soldiers cook up a
rudimentary meal during
World War I, circa 1916

The Early Years

A s Winston Churchill and Adolf Hitler were young men during World War I, it is worth considering their involvement to understand how they became the men they were in World War II.

At the outbreak of World War I, Winston Churchill was already a high profile military and political figure. He had been First Lord of the Admiralty since 1911 and introduced a number of important modernizing reforms. However, it was Churchill's idea to mount the disastrous Gallipoli Campaign, so he was forced to resign in 1915. Faced with having to rebuild his reputation, Churchill became an officer at the Western Front, where he took a proactive role and exposed himself to considerable danger. He had exhibited similar reckless daring at the Second Boer War some fifteen years before and it was this fearlessness and determination that would eventually lead the British people to put their faith in him during World War II.

Winston Churchill and General French walk their horses together on manoeuvres during World War I

Unlike Churchill, Adolf Hitler was yet to make a name for himself when World War I began. He volunteered to serve the German army and became a dispatch runner, seeing action in a number of major battles, including Ypres, the Somme, Arras and Passchendaele. For his bravery and injuries he was awarded the Iron Cross, Second Class in 1914 and First Class in 1918. Having invested so much enthusiasm and effort into the war, he was incensed when the Central Powers capitulated to the Entente and this catalyzed his nationalist ideology that would evolve into Nazism.

Intriguingly, Churchill and Hitler had similarities. They were both attracted to danger as an expression of machismo and both had forged reputations based on those experiences. Also, they both fancied themselves as artists and were competent amateurs at drawing and painting. The difference was that Hitler had wanted to become a professional artist, while to Churchill it was a cathartic pastime.

Adolf Hitler dressed in his field uniform
during World War I

Both men were certainly egotists, but they came from very different backgrounds and that made them very different as personalities. Churchill came from the British upper class and had a sense of entitlement and expectation, which is why he bent and broke the rules with impunity. Hitler had to climb the social ladder and deal with a fundamental sense of inferiority, which gave him his passion and drive to succeed, but also riddled him with hatred and prejudices. In power, Churchill saw himself honestly, as a flawed leader doing his best for his people. Hitler portrayed himself as a divinely chosen and faultless leader, but underneath he knew the truth, which is why he took his own life when he realized the unlikely game was up.

Corporal Adolf Hitler, right, with two other soldiers and a dog during his stay in a military hospital, WWI, Pasewalk, Pomerania

Trench Raids and Weapons

Due to the stalemate of trench warfare at the Western Front, soldiers were unable to advance. Day time assaults were suicidal, as the soldiers were cut down by machine gun fire as soon as they went over the top. As a result, night time raids became the modus operandi on both sides.

The objective was to black-up with burnt cork and cross no man's land undetected and then enter the enemy trench and dispatch as many of the foe as possible without being heard. This meant that noisy firearms were not to be used, unless their cover was blown and it made no difference. So hand weapons, such as bayonets, trench knives, Bowie knives and knuckle-dusters, were all used and rifles and pistols were kept in reserve.

A British soldier in a flooded dug-out in a front line trench near Ploegsteert Wood, Flanders, 1917

The principal strategy was to catch sentries
by surprise and stab them through the heart or
cut their throats, whilst preventing them from
shouting out and alerting others. Once the sentries
were dealt with, it was then possible to raid billets,
simply by lobbing grenades inside and making a
quick exit to avoid being caught in the explosion
and to escape before reserve soldiers arrived.
So, the initial stage of a raid would be silent, but
followed by the chaos of explosions and gunfire.

With any luck, the raiders would make it back
across no-man's-land to live another day, but there
was always the risk of being caught on barbed
wire or being shot by friendly fire. In an effort to
eliminate the possibility of being mistaken for the
enemy, raiders used passwords in order to let their
own sentries know who they were in the darkness.

Periscopes were often used by sentries to keep an
eye on no-man's-land without the risk of being
shot. If they suspected a raid might be immanent
then flares would be fired to illuminate the sky and
expose the raiders, so that machine gunners could
see their target and open fire.

Steel helmeted British soldiers in France practise
their attack as they hurdle an old trench

Two British soldiers waiting
for the signal to attack at
Ginchy, 1916

This tit-for-tat raiding was an on-going part of trench warfare and was encouraged by high command, because it prevented soldiers from losing their combative edge. The constant risk of being killed and challenge of having to kill, kept the troops psychologically tuned for the job in hand, in readiness for eventual movement in the frontline.

Italian alpinists defending an attack from a trench dug into the mountain

American troops
advancing on Cantigny,
France, 28th May 1918

The Flying Aces

A s World War I progressed, so did mechanization in the air. It wasn't long before fighter aeroplanes were manoeuvrable and reliable enough to partake in aerial dog-fights. The aeroplanes did not yet pose a significant threat to ground operations, except in a reconnaissance role, so pilots were waging a private battle for air superiority, partly motivated by the intelligence threat but also as a matter of pride.

Aeroplanes were conspicuous and they captured the imagination in a way unlike other machines of war. As a result, they possessed propaganda value and the pilots were regarded as courageous and romantic daredevils. In this rarefied atmosphere, the phenomenon of the flying ace was born and much exploited by the media of the era, on both sides. The flying ace came to personify the war effort from both the Allied and German perspectives, because the public was able to see a face and read a name, which represented all of those fighting at the Front.

American fighter pilot Eddie Rickenbacker, a commanding officer in the US 94th Aero Pursuit Squadron, poses next to his Nieuport 28 N6169 during World War I

A Sopwith Camel, 1917; being small and lightweight, represented the latest in fighter design at the time

Probably the most famous of all flying aces
is Manfred von Richthofen, who went by the
sobriquet Red Baron. This was because he flew
a distinctive bright-red Fokker Dr.1 triplane.
He chalked up eighty air combat victories, before
being killed by enemy fire whilst in the air near
the Somme in April 1918. He had a brother, Lothar
von Richthofen, who was also a flying ace, with
forty victories to his name by the end of the war.
Both were handsome and decorated young men,
making them very popular with the Teutonic
public. Other notable German flying aces include
Oswald Boelcke (40 victories) and Max Immelman
(15 victories).

The German approach to keeping tallies of air
combat victories was far more formal than that
of the Allies, which probably said something
about their ordered and serious approach to life in
general. British, French, Italian and US flying aces
were recognized, but they were celebrated more
modestly and their victory tally records are more
vague, as if it were not all that important. What
mattered was that they had five or more kills, as
that was sufficient to demonstrate that they had
prowess at the controls. After all, many pilots only
lasted a few flights before being shot from the skies
or crashing, so anyone who managed to both stay
alive and kill a few Huns was a hero regardless
of tally.

Manfred Von Richthofen

German flying ace Baron Manfred von Richthofen (The Red Baron) salutes in front of the officers and staff of Fighting Squadron No. 11 as they stand in formation

n fighter triplane Fokker Dr 1, plane of the
Manfred von Richthofen (T

German fighter triplane Fokker
Dr 1, plane of the Baron
Manfred von Richthofen (The
Red Baron)

243

Prisoners of War

During the course of World War I, many combatants found themselves captured by the enemy and held in POW (Prisoner Of War) camps. In all, about seven million were incarcerated between 1914 and 1918. As housing and feeding prisoners was an inconvenience and expensive, both in terms of resources and manpower, most prisoners of war were treated with general disdain and kept in squalid conditions with all expenses spared.

European nations had signed the Hague Convention in 1907, which stipulated that prisoners of war were to be treated humanely and that they were prisoners of the government, not the people. This was important, as it made it clear that the government would be held accountable for any inhumane treatment and torture. All of the main participating nations in World War I had signed the convention, except for the Turks, as the Ottoman Empire was part of Asia.

A German officer tying
up a Russian prisoner
of war, 1916

A concentration camp
for German prisoners of
war in Surrey

247

The Germans kept just short of a quarter of a
million Allied prisoners in about three-hundred
POW camps. Conditions were typically harsh, as
the Central Powers could ill-afford to divert much
of their war effort to maintaining and guarding the
camps. The officers and guards tended to be old or
second-rate soldiers, who were not fit for duty at
the frontlines. All aspects of prison life made the
experience a test of endurance. Food was poor,
sanitation was unhygienic, space was limited
and so on. This made the environment such that
physical and mental illnesses were commonplace.

The prisoners were, however, allowed to send and
receive letters from home, which was an important
psychological catharsis and gave them something
to focus on. The Red Cross provided modest
rations, but these were insufficient to sustain
health and life, so the prisoners relied on a lifeline
of food parcels sent by their loved ones.

A number of escapes and escape attempts occurred. Although there was the obvious benefit of being freed from prison conditions, many soldiers, especially officers, had a strong sense of duty and wanted to return to active service. Planning escapes also gave them something to think about to alleviate the tedium, and there was the additional satisfaction in knowing that escapes cost the Germans valuable time and effort in searching for them even if they failed to remain liberated.

Prisoners were also used to perform many kinds of work to assist in the war effort against their own people. As the war dragged on, the Central Powers had a drastic shortage of manpower, so the prison labour force became vitally important. Following the ceasefire on the Eastern Front, the Russian POWs were not released, because Germany could not afford to let go of any assistance in the renewed war effort on the Western Front.

Two German prisoners of war
imprisoned in a stable after
the Champagne offensive

Intelligence and Espionage

At the frontline in World War I, reconnaissance was the way most intelligence about the enemy was gathered. This was simply using vantage points, observation balloons, aeroplanes and so on to spy on the enemy's movements. This was done covertly if at all possible, so that the enemy was unaware that it had been compromised, but overt spying was also practiced, when aircraft would fly over and take photographs, for example.

Trench codes were also used at the Western Front, so that important information didn't fall into enemy hands during trench raids. The only problem was that code books were required to decipher incoming messages and to compose outgoing messages. This meant that code books would need to be very well hidden, or codes would need to be periodically changed. As a result, those at the front were often reluctant to bother with codes even though high command considered it a good idea. It was simply a difference in opinion over the practicality of using codes in real situations, where the perceived advantages could be lost by the time and inconvenience.

A German observer in the basket of a hot-air balloon using a camera for aerial reconnaissance

Away from the Front, espionage was rife on both sides, because it was useful to know about the bigger picture, such as major troop movements, supply routes and weapons' manufacture. For this reason, all participating nations had agents whose job it was to gather information and relay it back to those for whom it was useful. This led to double-agents too, who posed as friends but were actually working for the enemy by providing disinformation.

One of the most famous suspected agents was a woman called Mata Hari, a celebrated Dutch burlesque dancer, whose real name was Margaretha Zelle. Being Dutch, she was neutral and able to cross borders during the war, which she did frequently and was consequently questioned by the British counter-espionage team.

She was first suspected of working for the French, but then information came to light that implicated her as a German agent. When she went to trial the prosecution could not conclusively prove her guilt, but they stated that she was very likely to be responsible for the deaths of fifty thousand troops.

English observation balloon of the Royal Flying Corps

As a result she was executed by firing squad in October 1917, under the rationale that she was probably guilty anyway, and that her publicized death would serve as a sober reminder of the seriousness of furnishing the enemy with intelligence.

These days her trial would have collapsed, but the scandal happened at a crucial juncture in the war, when people were getting very weary of the rising death toll and looking for someone to blame.

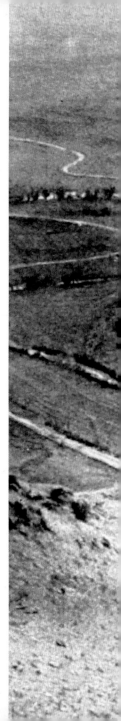

Reconnaissance in the gorges of the Rajec. An infantry sergeant observing the Prilep road from the Drenovo Pass, Serbia

Soldiers celebrating
World War I Armistice

Admission, Abdication and Armistice

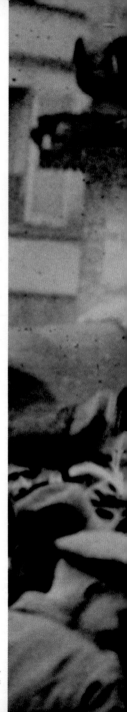

By late September 1918, it dawned upon the German high-command that the war at the Western Front was unwinnable. The hollow victory at the Eastern Front, due to the civil war in Russia, had been used by propagandists to make the German people think that victory at the Western Front was now an inevitable conclusion. In truth, the renewed effort in the west was too little too late. By that time, the Germans were critically short of manpower and resources, and they had provoked the US into joining the Allies. Despite their initial success at moving the frontline by implementing new tactics, they were a spent force and the tide had turned against them.

Crowds of people celebrating the signing by Germany of the armistice on November 11, 1918

ÉDITION DE PARIS

Le Petit Parisien

10 Cent.   **LE PLUS FORT TIRAGE DES JOURNAUX DU MONDE ENTIER** ★★ 10 Cent.

DIMANCHE
10
NOVEMBRE 1918

LE KAISER A CÉDÉ : IL ABDIQUE

Le kronprinz est déchu. - Une assemblée nationale fixera la Constitution allemande

Berne, 9 novembre.

Le service allemand de propagande annonce que le chancelier prince Max de Bade a publié la proclamation suivante :

L'empereur et roi a décidé d'abdiquer.

Le chancelier restera en fonctions jusqu'à ce que les questions se rapportant à l'abdication de l'empereur, à la renonciation du kronprinz au trône de l'empire d'Allemagne et du royaume de Prusse et à l'institution d'une régence soient réglées.

Il a l'intention de proposer au régent la nomination du député Ebert comme chancelier et le dépôt d'un projet de loi portant fixation immédiate d'élections générales en vue d'une Assemblée nationale allemande constituante, qui aurait pour tâche de déterminer définitivement la Constitution future du peuple allemand, y compris les éléments qui pourraient désirer entrer dans le cadre de l'empire.

Berlin, 9 novembre 1918.   *Le chancelier : Prince MAX DE BADE.*

---

révolution de la défaite brise toute l'armature impériale

Le chancelier, débordé, annonce un régent et veut passer la main à un socialiste

Mais quelles seront les surprises de demain ?

LA MARCHE VICTORIEUSE :
Tournai, Maubeuge, Mons, Hirson, Mézières

L'entrevue historique des plénipotentiaires allemands avec le maréchal Foch

---

LE CHANCELIER AVAIT DÉMISSIONNÉ DÈS VENDREDI

LA ROUMANIE SE LIBÈRE
Le général Coanda remplace M. Marghiloman

A grandes enjambées

On the 29th of September, Kaiser Wilhelm II received a communication from General Ludendorff recommending a ceasefire in anticipation that the Allies would soon break through the German lines and take the front eastward to Germany. By 5th October, Germany had asked to negotiate peace with the Allies, but the conditions, including the Kaiser's abdication and withdrawal to the German border, were considered too harsh, so Ludendorff had a change of heart.

By late October, revolution was in the air, as factions of the German military were beginning to turn against the monarchy in favour of a democratic government. As the situation escalated, the Kaiser was forced to abdicate by his own people and the Weimar Republic was announced on the 9th of November. Negotiations with the Allies were concluded at 5 am on the morning of the 11th of November, with the armistice to come into effect at 11am to provide enough time for the word to spread along the Western Front.

Newspapers report the abdication of William II, emperor of Germany, November 10, 1918

From the point of view of the German military, the war had come to a premature end due to the political revolution. Largely unaware that the political revolution had actually been a symptom of German attrition, they felt as if they had been prevented from fighting a war they were about to win, so their pride was deeply hurt and they sought people to blame. It was this sense of unfinished business that would prevail in the interwar years and give Adolf Hitler the platform upon which he would build the Nazi cause.

For a while, the new government of Germany was communist, and this is why Hitler was so anti-communist. His subjective view of the armistice made him believe that the communists were to blame for bringing the war to a close and preventing the Germans from having their glorious victory. Had he apprehended that the underlying cause was poor administration of finite German resources, then he might not have allowed history to repeat itself with his own blinkered strategic decisions during World War II.

Excited London citizens cheering in streets
and from atop double decker bus after news
of the World War I armistice signing is heard

The Socio-political Legacy

If we are to find something positive in the
wholesale slaughter of World War I, then it is
best to consider the revolutions and reforms that
it catalyzed in Europe and elsewhere in the world.
Above all else, it prompted the rise of the common
man in society, simply because so many had made
the ultimate sacrifice and so many families were
left affected by the war in one way
or another.

In Britain, the erosion of the class system had been
initiated and voting reforms allowed the masses to
have a much greater say in who should be elected
to government. Significantly, women over the age
of thirty were also allowed to vote for the first time
in the post-war election of December 1918. British
suffragettes had been actively campaigning before
the war, but had agreed to contribute to the war
effort in 1915 when it became apparent that the
conflict was going to last for some time.

Visiters walking around Tyne Cot Cemetery,
near Ypres, Belgium

Tyne Cot Cemetery, the largest Commonwealth war grave cemetery in
the world, near Ypres, Belgium

Due to the loss of so many young men, there was also a shortage of manpower in post-war Britain. This marked a social change, because those available to work had a greater say in terms of pay, working conditions and prospects for promotion. In effect, this ushered in the true middle-class, as Britain became a meritocracy, allowing people to climb the social ladder according to their skills and abilities. Prior to that, people very much belonged to the class in which they were born, so relatively few had the opportunity or wherewithal to become upwardly mobile.

Another aspect of the legacy of World War I was the early signs of empire disintegration. Many British colonies had taken part in the conflict and lost considerable numbers of people, yet there was no perceivable gain to be had from it. As a result, the seeds of independence were sown, because those populations realized that they would be better off governing themselves and making their own decisions. The brave new world was just around the corner.

British POWs being given refreshments on a London railway platform on their arrival back in Britain

Meanwhile, Russia was undergoing its transformation into a communist nation. The royal family had all been executed and the Bolsheviks had taken control under Lenin. The general Russian population had enough of living in poverty, while the aristocracy lived in luxury. Due to the interrelatedness of the European royal families, the inclusion of Russia in World War I had seemed like a cosying gesture on the part of the Tsar and Russian society was ripe for political revolution.

The picture shows the revolutionists on the second day of the Russian Revolution

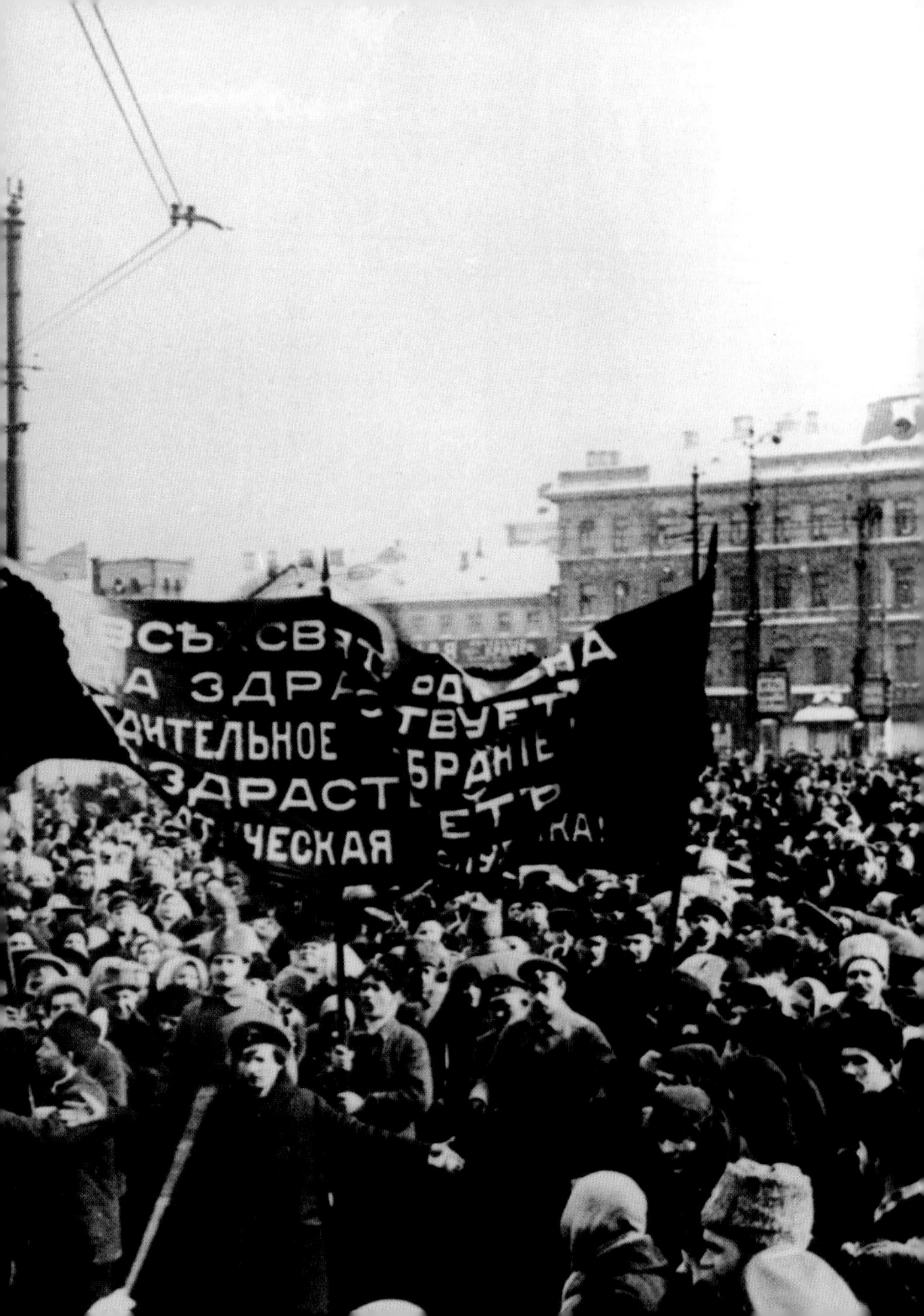
ВСЪ СВЯТ
А ЗДРА
ТВУЕТ
ТЕЛЬНОЕ
БРАНІЕ
ЗДРАСТ
ЧЕСКАЯ

An illustration of the Hall of Mirrors in the Palace of Versailles, published in 1871. This was the location for the signing of the Treaty of Versailles, Paris, 28th June 1919

The Ember Left Glowing

General John Pershing, who led the American Expeditionary Force in World War I, was very much against the idea of an armistice with Germany. He wanted to defeat the German army in no uncertain terms and warned that the Germans would only rise again if allowed to think that the war ended in a draw. So it was, that an ember was left glowing in the ashes, ready to be fanned back into flames.

The terms agreed for the armistice, which was officially signed at the Treaty of Versailles on 28th June 1919, were quite harsh on the Germans, to ensure that they were rendered unable to launch any new offensives. The result was economic collapse in post-war Germany and this only served to nurture resentment towards the Allied powers.

French Prime Minister Georges Clemenceau (left), US President Woodrow Wilson (centre) and British Prime Minister David Lloyd-George (far right) leaving the Palace of Versailles after signing the Treaty of Versailles, Paris, 28th June 1919

By 1920 the Nationalist Socialist Workers' (Nazi) Party had been established in Germany to counter the communist movement, held to account for the state of the nation at that time. Adolf Hitler became leader of the party in 1921 and happened to possess a gift for public speaking that captured the imaginations of many disillusioned Germans, who were seduced by the idea of Germany rising once again.

In addition, Hitler had developed resentment for Jews, because they seemed to be well off in relation to the rest of the population, but kept their wealth to themselves and seemed, in his view, disinclined to show benevolence. Thus, Hitler had his targets for vilification, which he would use to whip up a frenzy of hatred and blame. Communists and Jews were to be the pariahs of the German nation, enabling Hitler to provide his followers with a collective focus for their frustrations, which actually had nothing to do with the truth but served as a very effective political tool.

German dictator Adolf Hitler on board a ferry in the Baltic Sea, 1921

Hitler saluting at a Nuremberg rally, 1934

Adolf Hitler addresses
soldiers with his back
facing the camera at a
Nazi rally in Dortmund,
Germany, 1933

283

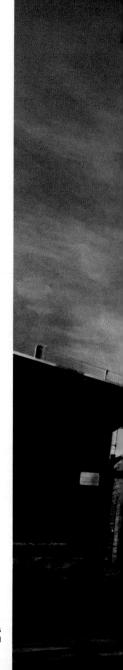

In order to give the Germans a sense of behavioural
cohesion, the Nazis also introduced notions of
Aryan purity and perfection by educating the
young with quasi-Darwinian ideas. This led to
the additional persecution of anyone who didn't
fit with the ideal. The physically disabled, the
mentally ill and those from other races and
religions were all on the list of undesirables.
As the Nazi party rose to power, so too did the
abominable persecution of Jews in Germany.

Between 1918 and 1939, Germany had lifted itself
from its knees and resolved to restore its own
pride by once again attempting to conquer Europe.
Pershing's prophecy had come true, only this time
it came with a far more dangerous ideology that
brainwashed the German army into believing it
belonged to the master race. In the end though,
it would be that delusion of superiority that would
lead to the fall of the Third Reich.

Entrance to Auschwitz-Birkenau, the infamous
concentration camp in Krakow, Poland

Adolf Hitler walks up
swastika-lined steps with
other party functionaries
during a mass rally,
Germany, 1934

Picture Credits

All images featured in this book are courtesy of Getty Images
© Getty Images

Cover image: The Print Collector / © Alamy Stock Photo

Endpapers: front, IWM / © Getty Images; back, Hulton Archive / Stringer
/ © Getty Images